grow with me

BEAN

CREATIVE EDUCATION · CREATIVE PAPERBACKS

Published by Creative Education
and Creative Paperbacks
P.O. Box 227, Mankato, Minnesota 56002
Creative Education and Creative Paperbacks are
imprints of The Creative Company
www.thecreativecompany.us

Design by Ellen Huber
Production by Travis Green
Art direction by Rita Marshall
Printed in Malaysia

Photographs by Alamy (Nigel Cattlin), Corbis (Alistair
Baker, Laura Berman, David Cavagnaro/Visuals
Unlimited, Gary J Weathers, Jeremy Woodhouse/
Holly Wilmeth), Dreamstime (Francois Lariviere,
Seksan Wangjaisuk), Shutterstock (Elena Elisseeva,
Massimiliano Gallo, Arto Hakola, holbox, Hurst Photo,
Imageman, juniart, Tukaram Karve, Madlen, Napat,
Naypong, Charles B. Ming Onn, Zeljko Radojko,
SandKumar, sima, smereka, Sponner, TAGSTOCK1,
wk1003mike, Peter Zijlstra)

Library of Congress Cataloging-in-Publication Data
Murray, Laura K.
Bean / Laura K. Murray.
p. cm. — (Grow with me)
Includes bibliographical references and index.
Summary: An exploration of the life cycle and life span
of beans, using up-close photographs and step-by-step
text to follow a bean's growth process from seed to
seedling to mature plant.

ISBN 978-1-60818-560-3 (hardcover)
ISBN 978-1-62832-161-6 (pbk)
1. Beans—Juvenile literature. 2. Beans—Life cycles—
Juvenile literature. I. Title. II. Series: Grow with me.
SB327.M88 2015
635.652—dc23   2014028004

CCSS: RI.3.1, 2, 3, 4, 5, 6, 7, 8; RI.4.1, 2, 3, 4, 5, 7; RF.3.3, 4

First Edition HC 9 8 7 6 5 4 3 2 1
First Edition PBK 9 8 7 6 5 4 3 2 1

TABLE OF CONTENTS

Beans are a type of legume (*leg-YOOM*). Legumes are plants with **pods**. People grow many kinds of beans to eat. They grow green beans, pinto beans, kidney beans, and more. Soybeans are a related bean. Farmers use a lot of soybeans in **livestock** feed.

Most beans are annual plants. That means they live for a year or less. Most beans grow best in warm weather. All beans need soil, water, and lots of sunlight, too.

4

People around the world call many types of legumes "beans."

5

6 *Young green beans have tender pods and very small seeds.*

Beans are flowering plants that produce pods. Seeds are inside the pods. Bean pods are flat and straight or curved and circular. Most pods are green, yellow, or even purple. Bean seeds can be many colors, like green, red, or black. Some are **speckled**.

Snap beans (like green beans) have pods that are soft enough to eat. Shell beans (like lima beans) and dry beans (like kidney beans) have tough pods. People eat only the seeds inside these types of pods. Shell beans have soft seeds, and dry beans have hard seeds.

Garden bean seeds are planted at least two inches (5.1 cm) apart.

8

A bean grows when a person plants the seed in the ground. For most beans, the temperature of the soil should be at least 60 °F (15.6 °C). But the soil can be cooler for soybeans and fava beans.

Rows of beans are planted in gardens or fields. Beans grow in large pots, too. Seeds should be planted 1 to 1.5 inches (2.5–3.8 cm) deep. They need eight hours of sunlight every day.

Farmers grow beans in long rows that provide proper light and moisture to the crops.

10 *Soybeans may be grown for their seeds or for the oil inside.*

A bean seed is dry. Inside the seed is an **embryo** (*EM-bree-oh*). The embryo is wrapped in a hard shell called a seed coat. Water softens the seed coat. Then the seed begins to **germinate** (*JER-mih-nate*).

The embryo bursts through the seed coat. The seed's root reaches down into the soil. It collects water for the plant. After 6 to 15 days, a stem and leaves push up through the ground. This new plant is called a seedling.

11

12 *The scientific name for a bean plant's seed leaves is cotyledons.*

At first, a seedling has just two round leaves. These are called seed leaves. They store food for the plant until it grows more leaves. The seed leaves fall off after a week or so.

A bean's leaves are shaped like ovals or hearts. Nodes are the places where the leaves connect to the stem. Leaves use sunlight, air, and water to make food for the plant.

13

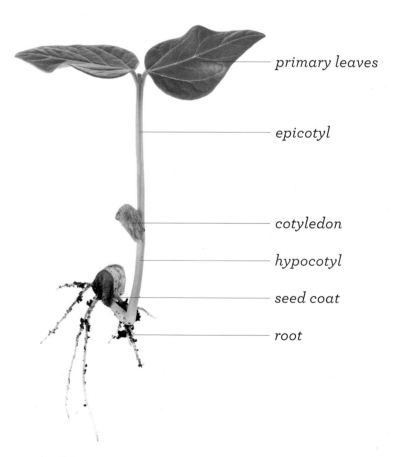

primary leaves

epicotyl

cotyledon

hypocotyl

seed coat

root

The flowers of green beans usually have five petals each.

14 A bean plant flowers 35 to 50 days after planting. Green bean flowers are white, yellow, pink, or purple. Scarlet runner beans have red and pink flowers.

The male part of a flower, called the stamen, sheds **pollen**. The pollen falls onto the female part of the flower, called the pistil. After the flower is **pollinated**, it becomes a tiny pod.

Many people grow
scarlet runner beans
mainly for the flowers.

15

16 *Green beans on poles take up less space than those on bushes.*

One bean plant often has more than 20 pods. Soybeans can have 80 pods! Inside the pods, seeds grow quickly. Warm weather can help some types of bean pods **ripen** in a week.

Some beans grow on bushes. The bushes are one to two feet (30.5–61 cm) high. Other beans grow on vines. They are called pole beans because they need a pole, fence, or string to climb. Pole bean vines can grow to be 15 feet (4.6 m) tall!

17

Fresh green beans make a snapping sound when broken.

Beans are picked at different times. Green beans can be picked before they are fully grown. Their firm pods are about four inches (10.2 cm) long. The seeds inside are still small.

As a bean pod gets older, its skin becomes tough. Its seeds get bigger. Lima beans are picked when the pod is green. Black turtle beans are picked when their pods are dry and brown. People do not eat the dried up pods.

18

People eat the seeds of black turtle beans (opposite) or the whole pod of green beans (pictured).

19

20

Top soybean-producing states include Iowa, Illinois, and Minnesota.

Fuzzy soybean pods turn a yellowish-brown before harvest.

After picking, some beans grow new pods. The plant might produce pods several more times! People like to plant beans in a new place every two to three weeks. That way, they will have a long **harvest** of beans.

Growers use machines called combines to harvest big fields of soybeans. The combine separates the pod from the seed.

21

Many beans cannot survive a **frost**. Very wet soil can make beans rot or crack. If the weather is too hot and windy, bean pods become hard and stringy. They might even stop growing.

Insects such as beetles and aphids eat beans. Deer and rabbits like bean plants, too. Sometimes beans get sick with dark spots. But growers try to keep their beans healthy.

22

Black bean aphids feed on plant stems, pods, and leaves.

Frost may turn a bean
plant's leaves dark
green to black.

23

24

Fresh green beans can be refrigerated up to five days.

Beans are good sources of iron and **fiber**. People like to eat crunchy snap beans raw. The pods can be cooked or steamed like vegetables, too. They can even be **preserved** in cans or frozen!

Shell beans and dry beans are mixed into salads and soups or used in other dishes. Red kidney beans are **poisonous** until they are soaked in water and boiled. Soybeans can be made into soy milk and cheese.

25

People have grown beans for thousands of years. Long ago, beans grew **wild** in the Middle East. Most of the beans people eat today were first **cultivated** in Central America. Now people around the world grow and eat beans.

26

Beans can be used for more than just food. Soybeans help make soap, oils, plastics, fuel, and ink. Often, products that are made from beans are better for the environment.

Some dried beans must be soaked in water before cooking and eating.

27

When the bean is done producing pods, it withers and dies. The same plant will not grow again the next year. In the spring, a new bean seed will be planted. It will grow pods and make delicious beans for everyone to enjoy.

28

Bush green beans hide under the leafy layers of the plant.

Soybeans are ready for harvest when the pods dry and leaves drop.

A seed is planted in the ground.

In 6 to 15 days, the seed germinates.

The seedling grows for several weeks.

A bean plant flowers 35 to 50 days after planting.

The plant self-pollinates.

After 7 to 20 days, pods appear.

 Bean pods ripen for a week or longer.

Beans are picked 50 to 100 days (or more) after planting.

The bean plant dries up and dies.

cultivated: *planted by people; not wild*

embryo: *the part of a seed that grows into a plant*

fiber: *a substance found in food that keeps the digestive system healthy*

frost: *a time of colder weather when ice forms and plants stop growing*

germinates: *starts to grow*

harvest: *a collection of crops*

insects: *animals that have six legs and one or two pairs of wings*

livestock: *farm animals such as chickens and cows*

pods: *parts of plants that hold seeds*

poisonous: *causing death or illness*

pollen: *a yellow powder made by flowers that is used to fertilize other flowers*

pollinated: *fertilized, causing seeds to grow*

preserved: *kept in its original state*

ripen: *become ripe, or ready for picking and eating*

speckled: *spotted with color*

wild: *living on its own; not grown by people*

31

DLTK: Jack and the Beanstalk Coloring Pages
http://www.dltk-teach.com/rhymes/beanstalk/color.htm
Print out coloring pages from "Jack and the Beanstalk."

PBS Kids: ZoomSci Germination Activity
http://pbskids.org/zoom/activities/sci/germinator.html
Learn how to grow your own beans from seeds.

Note: Every effort has been made to ensure that the websites listed above are suitable for children, that they have educational value, and that they contain no inappropriate material. However, because of the nature of the Internet, it is impossible to guarantee that these sites will remain active indefinitely or that their contents will not be altered.

READ MORE

Hibbert, Clare. *The Life of a Bean.*
Chicago: Raintree, 2005.

Royston, Angela. *Life Cycle of a Bean.*
Des Plaines, Ill.: Heinemann Interactive Library, 2009.

32

INDEX